Ghost Guest

Ghost Guest

poems

Rachel Hadas

RAGGED SKY PRESS
PRINCETON, NEW JERSEY

Copyright © 2023 Rachel Hadas
All rights reserved
Published by Ragged Sky Press
270 Griggs Drive, Princeton, NJ 08540
www.raggedsky.com

Library of Congress Control Number: 2023932024
ISBN: 978-1-933974-52-1
Cover and book design: Dirk Rowntree
Cover and author photo: Shalom Gorewitz
Printed in the United States of America
First Edition

For ghosts and guests,
the living and the dead

Contents

I

Piece by Piece | 3
Rainbow Parfait | 4
The Head of the Table | 5
A Long Time | 6
460 Riverside Drive | 7
Weathering | 9
Holding Their Arms Out | 10
Forest and Trees | 11
The Trick | 12
The Missing Line | 13
The Archivist | 14
Opening the House | 15
The Nest | 16
This March Afternoon | 18
Early, Late | 20
Stained Glass, Hailstorm, Rainbow | 21
Flowers in the River | 22
Fingernails | 23
Stowaways | 24
Ethical Dative | 25
Blue | 26
Threshold and Mirror | 27
Tea and a Dream | 29
Mervyn Peake | 30
Studying the Maze | 32
Left-Handed | 33
Kitten by Foujita | 34
Snow Sculpture, Riverside Park | 35
Tracks in Snow | 36
Riders, Parthenon Frieze | 37

Raw Jute | 38
Repurposing | 39
White Designs | 40

II

The Gift | 43
Lyric Leap | 44
Ovid's *Metamorphoses* | 45
Under the Floorboards | 47
Nap | 48
Messages | 49
Waking Up | 50
Tiger Stripes | 51
Brooding on Cities the Morning after a Cavafy Evening | 53
Plato at the Crossroads | 54
Sustainable Systems | 56
In Aulis: One Version | 58
Among the Taurians | 59
The Spark | 61
Teaching the *Iliad* | 62
Teaching the Tigers | 63
Who If I Cried | 64
Gradus ad Parnassum | 66
Liminal | 67
The Last Lecture Hall | 68
Tones of Meaning | 70
The Equation | 72
Waiting in Line for the Disney Show | 73
Visiting My Office 12/6/21 | 75
Ghost Guest | 76
A War by Any Other Name | 77

Acknowledgments | 79

I

Piece by Piece

> *All you grasp will be thrown away.*
> *All you hoard will be utterly lost.*
> –*Tao Te Ching, 44,* translated by Ursula K. LeGuin

I've practiced the poetics of space,
but there's a sequel: empty spaces
have a resounding poetry.
I'm standing, skimming through the Bs.
On the shelf near Bachelard,
Keith Basso: *Wisdom Sits
in Places.* Sits in empty places.
While it's easy, study the hard.
We've heard about the art of losing;
passing on is also choosing.
Things are in motion, fast or slow.
Clouds keep sailing through the sky.
Holding on makes nothing stay.
Give things permission to go.
Touch with gentleness, release,
and rooted objects will break loose,
a landslide that gathers speed
and leaves a brightness in its wake,
a lacy layer of memories
like foam lines scribbled on a beach.
This was Vermont. And here was Greece.
For the time left, what do I need?
What to take? What not to take?
Little by little, page by page,
let me give myself away.
Each addition to one's age
asks for subtraction. It is time
to be packing. Travel light.
What is the final appetite?
What is there I will not let go?

Rainbow Parfait

At the end of every summer,
Labor Day looming, school about to begin,
the family used to go to the Columbia Faculty Club
for dinner our first night back.
Air conditioning. Clinking ice.
Waiters in buff jackets.
View from the nineteenth floor of Butler Hall
out over Morningside Park.
What we talked about,
our father and mother and my sister and I,
all hot and tired after the eight, nine, ten-
hour drive down from Vermont,
is lost to the melt of memory.
The ritual dessert, though, sticks with me:
Rainbow Parfait, a multi-colored column
of sherbet stacked in a tall frosted glass
and topped with a maraschino cherry.
You had to poke and dig to get to the bottom.
Even the long-handled spoon was cold.

A lot of life feels horizontal.
Time stretches out and you can look ahead.
Lately, though, before I fall asleep,
my impulse is to tunnel back and down.
It is possible
to be the archaeologist of one's own past,
as if the sleeper, wakened now, alert,
was perched at the top of a trench
peering at something shining down below
and excavating down, down, down
through the strata of decades
with a long-handled spoon.

The Head of the Table

Not too long after my father died,
I began to forget him in motion.
I did retain a picture of him sitting
at the head of the table. Writing? No.
He must have written his books in his locked office.
Once each book was almost done, my mother
went down on her hands and knees on the living room rug
and sorted index cards. My father sat
at the head of the table and bounced me on his knee.
He was a toaster, I was a slice of bread.
He popped me up and buttered me all over.

The last page of *Walden* tells of *a strong and beautiful bug*
emerging from the *leaf of an old table*
which had stood in a farmer's kitchen for sixty years.
What beautiful and winged life, asks Thoreau,
may unexpectedly come forth?
A memory I thought had taken flight
has fluttered back to the table where it was born
where I now sit and write.

A Long Time

At the massive table in the dining room
my mother wrote brief essays
on each of her Latin students' report cards.
She was so good at finding synonyms
for "industrious" or "imaginative" or "lazy"
that her colleagues regularly asked her
to come up with lists of adjectives for them.
When I was small, I liked to hide under that table.
Smug in the belief I was invisible,
I could peek out and see
the grownups' legs and feet.
I was semi-hidden, like the owl
concealed in a fold of Alma Mater's
voluminous bronze robes
as she sat enthroned in front of Low Library.
The owl was an open secret.

On our small television (black/white; grainy),
the Hungarian Revolution was in progress.
I crept down the long winding hall
to the living room to hear.
Would there be a war?
"Don't worry, honey," said my mother,
who always told the truth.
"Things have been this way for a long time."

460 Riverside Drive

We lived on the ground floor. The doorman Earl
sat in the lobby. From our living room
through the wall we could hear
Earl's explosive sneezes loud and clear.
The knob of our apartment's front door
was big and brass, and Earl would vigorously
grasp and twist it, and with rag and smelly polish
noisily buff that knob until it gleamed.
It always gleamed. I knew
that brass polish was poison.
From our side of the door
the knob would visibly
turn as Earl twisted it, apparently
of its own accord,
untouched by human hand.
Visitors didn't understand.
Who was out there?
What ghostly messenger
was rattling away unseen
on the other side of the door?
Who, sent from where, was trying to get in?
The only polite thing was to ignore
the uncanny energy.
A lifetime later, it is clear to me,
or at least less murky:
I understand
Earl as a harbinger
from an undiscovered land.
White gloves and can of polish; courtesy.
"Don't fall down, now!" he'd admonish me.
Why should I fall? I wondered. I was five,
six, seven. I was agile and alive.
I roller-skated up and down
outside Grant's Tomb or on Riverside Drive.
It was the old ladies (these were the Fifties)
teetering along on their high heels,

hatted and gloved, with seams
in their stockings, and with glassy-eyed
fox furs draped over their massive chests,
who might fall down, not me.
Was it because it would have been
rude to warn them
that Earl kept warning me?
Mortality
has caught up with those ladies and with him,
rattled their doorknobs (it was time); gone in.
That lobby was so cold in wintertime,
I still remember:
the stiff wind off the river
so strong that neither Earl nor any tenant
could shut the outer door at all.
Eventually, Earl, everyone will fall.

Weathering

My mother had, I thought,
when I was growing up,
a uniform smooth surface like a rock
polished by waves. Or like
a flight of steps worn concave
at the center of each tread
she had been hollowed out.
This weathering, it took me years to see,
was neither luck nor personality.
Motherhood and years wear women down.
Either can alone;
but motherhood, although it saves no one,
mitigates the wear and tear somehow
with kindness—or with blindness. Take my hand
before we both are ground back into sand.

Holding Their Arms Out

Ghosts stand on the far bank,
holding their arms out,
yearning for the far shore.

Hours lean forward, proffering their gifts.
People lean forward, questions poised on their lips.
They want an answer, but there is no answer.
Each answer generates another question.

I always fear and hope and fear
that nothing will change.
My fear is always unrealized.
My hope is always disappointed.

A patch of moonlight
catches a cardigan draped
over the back of a chair.

Forest and Trees

Pacing the greyish green
corridor of a May
long as the slowest childhood,
I brush aside the drooping boughs to reach
a veil of intricate
and ramifying ways
to find you. Or to lose you? I forget.
Were you the habitat
through which all this cool spring
I strode? I left no stone unturned; each leaf
might signal hidden life.
I tramped up every glistening avenue,
threaded the season's maze as if
there was a destination I knew,
as if I'd reach a goal when I broke through
the stubborn undergrowth and clinging mist,
forgetting you inhabited all this,
forgetting all the greenery I so
impatiently pushed back was also you.

The Trick

I thought of it the other day,
a book my mother made with me.
We pressed wildflowers and fastened them
to pages marked with each flower's name
in my staggering child's script.
The daisy and buttercup we scotch-taped,
and Black-eyed Susan and Queen Anne's Lace,
Devil's Paintbrush, cinquefoil
(I think that I could name them all):
their dewy gold, though turned to dust
powdering the brittle page, then lost
to years that fade and dull and dry,
is vivid still in the mind's eye,
which is the eye with which I look
at that bulging little book.
I see its pages, eye-ease green,
though I won't see the book again.

Time in its passage helps me see
the law of mutability
apply its riddling decree:
what's perishable, fragile, lost
may be precisely what will last.
This one small notebook (Q.E.D.)
can hold the wealth of summers past
because all summers disappear.
Buttercups, daisies, that July,
my mother's presence—where are they?
Gone where they can't be taken away.
Gone with the snows of yesteryear.
The treasures of metonymy,
the riches of synecdoche,
their elegant economy,
their magical recovery
which captures a contingency
and tucks a golden memory
into a perfect private place
which never takes up any space:
this is the trick of poetry.

The Missing Line

As I slipped into sleep, my mother
recited the second line
of a couplet. I knew it rhymed,
but the first line was gone.

Not that I can remember
the second line, the line she quoted, either.
I was adrift. I only knew
that I missed my mother.

But missing my mother
was neither the first line
nor the second line.
It was the refrain.

My women friends, my sister:
it is their refrain too.
We say it and we sigh it and we know.
I waited for the missing line.

As I breathed the night in, this came back:
I had also been slipping into sleep
that same afternoon, as two tall women
read their poetry in a white tent.

And as the brunette and the blonde took turns,
I'd closed my eyes, and the unfinished couplet
swam before my gaze.
Then I was back in the tent

trying to pay attention to one more
retelling of a myth.
Persephone. Demeter.
The daughter and the mother.

The mother and the daughter.
The couplet incomplete,
a lifetime's task
to finish, never finished.

The Archivist

Rummaging all morning elbow-deep
in old letters, journals, manuscripts:
scraps surface. Phrases spin into fresh contexts.
Unanchored names seek faces.
Unlabeled faces look around for names.
Each rereading supersedes the last one
in order to make room for all the versions
layered into palimpsests. Stronger, stranger memories
make their way to the top of the pile
as if they were virgin pages in a notebook
whose pristine leaves are yellowing with age.

Opening the House

Mouse droppings in the postcard box
and other traces, other tracks
legible and illegible.
What layers of secrets sleep beneath
those dainty prints across the sill?
Always, the first day back, some wraith
reappears—benign but still…

My cousin's drinking Liquid Death.
And as he drains this mortal draught,
a déjà vu goes rippling by.
Can all of this be a replay,
the present as an aftermath,
drinking death from a tall green can,
arriving at the end of May?

We start to put the garden in.
A dark snake slides between two rocks.
Hush: peal of wind chimes, faint and sweet.
Also paradisiacal:
lilies of the valley at my feet.
But if I stopped, if I knelt down
to drink their sweet, sharp fragrance in,

my greed would break the fragile spell.
Let the perfume arrive by air,
a subtle ghost, as I move on
to dig some tool out of the barn.
Always distracted and en route,
we find by losing, by mistake.
One tiny typo—see?—unlocks

muse droppings in the postcard box.

The Nest

Late in my father's life,
a phoebe built her nest

high on the same front porch
where I am sitting now.

The repository
of an ongoing story—

so many iterations,
so many alterations,

so many generations—
this whole house is a nest.

I think it was his last
summer. But memory

is a tattered tapestry,
delicate as lace,

sagging, full of holes
through which slip most details.

I know it was this place.
The year I can't quite say.

But I can see today
another phoebe's nest

tucked under the porch roof.
Recursiveness of life:

where's easier than when.
My father is long gone.

The bird is here again—
the same and not the same,

near where her ancestor
some sixty years before

sat on a nest in turn.
If I make no noise

I see her, motionless
guardian of her house

until her brood can fly.
Then she too flies away.

My son has grown and flown.
Visions go and come.

But here she is today.
And I am here to see.

This March Afternoon

> *Something in the light of this March afternoon*
> *Recalls that first and dazzling one...*
> —James Merrill, *"A Tenancy"*

Recurring seasons fold time up
and seem to move it back.

Something in the light,
the penetrating light of early March:

this is the time of year the sun
slides around the apartment

and pours into the dining room
from a new angle every afternoon.

This is the time of year
my son at thirteen months

made his careful way toward
the sunbeam at the window.

Sun slides—but no, it doesn't.
The earth, we have been told, moves round the sun.

So much yet to unlearn,
my son, who has grown up, wrote recently.

Year by year the cycle starts again:
the angle of the sun

and a child at the window
looking up at the light.

The first word he spoke
as his grandmother carried him

down the long hall of the apartment
and he looked up over her shoulder

at the fixture on the ceiling
was *Light! Light!*

Early, Late

In June, the season being late,
we caught the apple blossoms' pink and white,
the purple of the lilacs, dark and light,
the lilies of the valley, sweet,
hard to see underfoot.
A cold spring slowed
their burgeoning. We'd come
early, to try to get the garden in,
but poised to pack and turn around again
to wish your mother a final goodbye.
This would be her last spring.
Or would it? Maybe not.
As if we could foresee, foretell,
let alone control.
Trees know to blossom,
flowers bloom on schedule.
We didn't have to leave.
We saw it all.
She died that fall.

Stained Glass, Hailstorm, Rainbow

F. G. 1925–2019

Twilight, dim hour. So how can things look clearer?
And yet they do. See—lost forms and faces.
October dusk: a beacon and a mirror.

Tilt the frame. A flash surprises you.
The stained-glass window of the synagogue
next door is glowing: red, gold, blue.

Change the angle and reframe the story.
A burst of hailstones rattling the pane—
even the weather is an allegory.

Once a life's over, spans of time and space
shrink the old self—cut it down to size
and set the person firmly into place

even as old memories morph to new
and how we read the narrative keeps changing.
I thought we understood this, I and you,

but we'd forgotten. Hints and clues and dreams—
an open door lets in a blade of light
stained with radiance. Nothing's what it seems.

The funeral: out of a clear blue sky
as at a signal everyone looked up:
a slice of rainbow shimmering suddenly.

Flowers in the River

Look! Red flowers (where did they come from?)
floating, petals, leaves, stems, thorns and all,
down the river that bisects the dream.

Death skews space. The matriarchal home
teeters: what once was center now a hole
brimful of flowers (but where did they come from?).

Clans gather. Generations in the sun,
sharing deckchairs, watch the flow and spill,
the running river, conduit of dreams,

death and birth, the many and the one.
Look: a cemetery on a hill.
Wreath, bouquets—where did they all come from?

The march of change, our come-and-go, the drum-
beat is incessant. Yet it's possible
to scoop a stillness from this rushing stream.

The face I recognize, but not the name.
Time is spilling like a waterfall.
These red flowers must have floated down
currents pulsing at the pace of dream.

Fingernails

Vanessa Redgrave thought whatever
separates life and death
is tiny as the sliver of a fingernail.
She said this not in mourning nor acceptance
but matter-of-factly. The occasion
was the tenth anniversary of her daughter's death.
The topic was mortality.

Fingernail. I remembered Hopkins' "Moonrise, June 19, 1876":
*I woke in the midsummer not-to-call night, | in the white and the walk
    of the morning:*
*The móon, dwindled and thinned to the fringe | of a fingernail held to
    the cándle,*
Or páring of páradisïácal fruit...

A mother's thoughts about the loss of her daughter
rendezvoused with a poetic fragment
in a kind of moonlit tryst, a meeting halfway
between nowhere and everywhere,
as the mind is everywhere and nowhere.
Grief slides into an ache that spreads and loops
into the rhythm of our mortal days:
precarious contingencies;
that tiny sliver praise.

Stowaways

Grief, love, memory,
triple abstractions, flew down south with me,
stowaways tucked briskly out of sight
until the ocean breeze turned like a key,
opened their cramped luggage, set them free.
Abstract no longer, they reminded me
I had had them with me all along,
but coded as the sun behind a cloud.
"Please stay,"
I said to them days later as we flew
(a narrow blaze of crimson in the sky)
back to the mainland. Their reply:
"Where were we all this time if not in you?"

Ethical Dative

We the living do for the dead
what they can no longer do
either for themselves or for us.
Grammar of deficits. Ethical dative. *For.*
For you, on your behalf, instead of you.
Cui bono? To your advantage. For your sake.
Because you are here but you no longer can.
Because you are no longer here.
Spring torrents carve out a new course for the river.
We the living do it for the dead.
Grammar of deficits. Ethical dative. *For.*
Because you are here and you no longer can.
Because you are no longer here.
Because.

Blue

When my son was two,
taken to the country for the first time
and held up to admire the rural view,
what did he see?
He told us: too much blue.
"I don't like those blue mountains," he said.

Looking at the powder-corpsy blue
walls of my Athenian apartment,
"Blue is a thirsty color," J. decreed.
Those two would have agreed.
But those two comments were so long ago.
My son is grown. My friend is dead.

Threshold and Mirror

for Langdon Hammer and James Merrill

If merely to read the massive biography
of a poet is arduous, then to write
it beggars the imagination. To stand
both close and far, to look forward and back,
to measure experience through the mirror
of pages, poems, letters...Poised at the threshold

of such a life, a chronicle features several thresholds
including the biographer's,
who sometimes peers into the cloudy mirror
of his own past and writes
in a crabbed cipher like Leonardo's. Back-
ward slanting letters stand

facing the past. Or else the writer stands
hesitant at this undertaking's threshold:
invited once, will he be welcomed back?
Not every biographer
completes the love letter he may have begun by wanting to write.
The documents he assembles yield a mirror,

but who will be reflected in that mirror?
So many shards of mosaic. I once stood
at the bottom of an Athenian staircase: right
above me waited my host, the poet. Threshold
into a chapter of my youthful biography
I perceive only now I'm looking back.

Books can be read either from front to back
or "like a Hebrew book" (Longfellow): mirror-
reversal of events. Biography
too can be understood
end to beginning. Advance over the threshold
and then retreat and start to read. Or write.

This book's each sentence strives to get things right.
The word flies forth and cannot be called back.
From birth to death is not a single threshold
but countless arches, wilderness of mirrors,
no right reflection no matter where you stand.
The brave biographer

takes a stand, traces a range of thresholds
wavering in a lifetime's hall of mirrors.
Death took the poet. This bio brings him back.

Tea and a Dream

in memory of James Merrill

One eye open, on its little island
in the hotel moat, a green lagoon,
an alligator loiters. Four o'clock:
tea in the lobby with my hungry son.
Darjeeling, scones, meringues: but you are gone.
Pennies tossed into the fountain splash.
What do we wish for? Hush.

It is too late for thanks.
Repayment, rather—in what mortal coin?
You blow toward us in the soft Gulf breeze,
you shine on us in fitful springtime sun,
dismembered into myriad legacies,
scattered among the elements. You're gone,
an absence palpitating in my dream.

A black glass elevator,
sliding down the outside of a building,
shudders to a halt on the ground floor.
The passengers, all poets, getting out,
look at one another. It is dawn.
Has there been a party? You are gone.
Through avenues still silent we move off

in different directions
toward separate obligations
that await us—families, jobs, and time,
a lifetime's sum of days
on this strange foundation. You are gone.
The black box, emptied of its cargo, light,
rides again to a Parnassian height.

Mervyn Peake

He learned the alphabet of arch and aisle
roaming the boundless castle that was home.
Arcades and corridors and battlements
rounded back on themselves, dead-ending, lost.
Unclear if there was anything called sky.
Friendly places—attic, open book—

led nowhere. Or the meaning of the book
burned with the library. Smoke scrolled up the aisle.
The roof came off. Under a changing sky
successive interpretations of home
shimmered into focus, then were lost.
Allegory: what this may have meant.

A girl named for a flower leaned over a battlement.
On a table behind her in the attic, a book
was open to a poem. Then her place was lost.
Ritual processions down an aisle
of venerable observance: this meant home.
She craned to see the color of the sky:

buttresses, but for years there had been no sky.
When the weather broke, it flooded the battlements.
Way to feel safe in a perilous home:
curl up bodily inside a book;
explore a cave in a confected isle;
wander through a fortress. For all lost

girls' or boys' stories trace what they have lost
from toys in the attic to dreams of a carefree sky.
Azure childhood. Royal riddles. I'll
try to explain what every gargoyle meant,
explicate each bright carving in this book:
weird holidays, the templates of a home.

Does the imagination make its own home?
Can we recognize meaning once it's lost?
Does life unfold inside or outside the book
whose every page presents a private sky?
You do it too now: scale each battlement
or set the figures marching up the aisle

tangled with isle, home, sky
and what each meant, lost in the labyrinth
of his enormous book.

Studying the Maze

The maze's heart: to find what you had lost
or fled from: tarnished key
crossing an arrow in an iron ring;
twinned red birds both fluttering their wings
toward a center hooked to heaviness.
One beggar's empty hat: oh help, oh give!
One peacock feather, wrong side up, opaque.
One tiny silver spoon. We must be fed.
Turn back the way you came, and turn again:
what you grappled with you finally meet
face to face in the labyrinth. And yet
stubborn opacity, an empty rune,
palimpsest to be interpreted,
faint inscriptions visible, then gone.

To parse the patterning by candlelight:
flames flicker, sheathing our shared concentration.
Can scattered symbols yield their secrets up?
Dream-like, the tenses of a divination
mime and masquerade, a hall of mirrors:
is was will be: which? So we lean in,
looking if not for an epiphany
at least a modest gleam of clarity,
health, renewal, change. And silently
each of us turns to their own deity
and in their private idiom starts to pray.

Left-Handed

Writing left-handed led
to wanting to paint too
or wanting to paint instead.
There could no longer be
any doubt: I saw
how swiftly poems flew
from me (and still can fly)
so freely I forgot
what it was I said
or rather what I wrote,
let alone what I meant
and whether it was true.
Let the left hand, then, write
and let the right hand paint?
More effort and less speed,
less spontaneity—
might these signify
more sincerity?
Left-handed, might I be
at one remove from my
pulse of anxiety?
More meaning, moving slow?
Color in place of line?
Ambidextrously
I pick up brush and pen.

Kitten by Foujita

Pen-and-ink kitten: rendering of some
kitten long grown up, grown old, long dead
(the drawing's from a century ago)
but also ours, the kitten that we know.
The way one unsheathed claw
protrudes from a curved paw;
the feathered tail;
the halo of soft white around the fur—
all these belie the two-dimensional,
pounce from the page, stretch, purr.
Believe this kitten's nothing more than flat
marks on paper; that
these words are merely blobs of black on white.
Then stroke the fictive kitten
with a touch as light
as Foujita's brush.
It's sleeping.
Hush.

Snow Sculpture, Riverside Park

What does it remind me of,
this creature patted out of snow,
lordly and lonely on a height,
surveying layers of sloping white
and children coasting down below?
Front paws crossed, tail curled behind,
muzzle already a bit blurred
by mittened hands or wind or rain—
some sort of snowman? Not at all.
Leonine, sphinxlike, ageless, sober,
stately yet ephemeral
here on its Cyclopean wall,
it turns away from the beholder
and toward the river, as the park
fades from snow-light into dark.
And now the memory rises: lean,
tensile, poised, streamlined by time,
the lions at Delos, in the glow
of Cycladic sun. Or snow.

Tracks in Snow

Not quite invisible, this braid
crossing the field like a silent road.
But illegible: a flurry
of scampering lightly etched on white
as afternoon thickens into night,
vanishing where the trees begin,
shadows at the edge of sight.
Scrabbling on snow,
where did they go,
those light and tiny paws and tail?
What wild creature made this trail?
What intention, fear, or need?
What semaphore we cannot read?
Instinct urged them toward the dark.
Gravity left this fragile mark
barely brushed on a crust of snow.
We'd sink in if we tried to follow,
trampling on the tracery
left by whatever passed this way.
Observe the tracks that lead away,
the freeze, the melt, the changing sky.
Notice the pattern. Let it go.

Riders, Parthenon Frieze

These riders have almost no space,
caracoling from A to B,
wrist shoulder elbow hoof and knee,
the horses rearing back in place,

almost no space but endless time,
sheltered from weather, nervously
grouped in close proximity,
their cluster here a kind of home.

Where are they going? You can see
light strike the faces; they move on
out of the shadows toward dawn.
Or is that radiance sun on stone?

All of them pointed the same way,
a muscled chest, a close-clipped mane,
a mantle flung over an arm,
quivering, eager, barely reined

in. Beyond vagaries of flesh,
laughter and joking, heat and flies,
manure left steaming in the dust,
their stillness is a silent praise

distilled and captured here, contained,
snatched from time and carved and caught,
life in its restless readiness
and what remains and what does not.

Raw Jute

Ibrahim Mahama, Accra, March 6, 2016

I have changed the space with what I've done.
From nothing, I made something happen there.
Ibrahim, a soft-spoken young man,
answered a question. It was asked again;
possibilities hung in the air.
The bridge was still a bridge when he was done,
but strangely draped. The struggle must go on.
Our silent past has left a throbbing scar
my work wraps up, continued the young man.

Nothing can be understood alone.
What's close recedes; what's distant now looks near.
Dorm, railway station, theater…What I've done
is hang a roof with sackcloth, underline
the mystery hidden in a public square
by hiring women from around the town
to stitch old sacks together. One by one
these form a garment that a space can wear.
Buildings breathe because of what I've done.

We look more closely when things disappear.
Colonial leavings—cocoa, charcoal, corn—
sift down, miasmic. Where there's smoke, there's fire.
Through solid structures what deep tremors run,
map of a struggle won and lost and won?
A few days later this brown shroud is gone,
a dream you wake from. Had it ever been?
Tell me, Ibrahim said, what I've done.
Explain what my mysterious mantles mean.

Repurposing

Nubuke Foundation, Accra

The pieces in this gallery
challenge us to name what they've become.
Everything here has been patched together
out of disassembled elements
jumbled, then reunited to some new
role or function. Fabric drapes a wall
and turns it to a canopy where past
bundles with future. Or take this mannequin,
a bride whose skirt is shredded plastic bags
elegantly tailored into tutu.
Her train is trash bags, heavier, glossy black.
After the art gallery, the beach.
Smoke of fish grilling, or of garbage burning.
The Gulf of Guinea's water, bathtub-warm.
Gentle breakers, lace and cream and foam,
wave upon wave deliver
their dowry of waste.

White Designs

Henry Vaughan's poem "Childhood"
makes mysterious mention
of "those white designs which children drive."
Squinting at the syntax,
I'm wondering: who does the driving here?
Do the children steer
white vehicles, or is it the designs
that propel them—are they the passengers?
Either way, the phrase,
with its push-me pull-you sense, rings true
enough. And in the way that poems have
of answering questions posed by other poems,
or if not answering, then at least extending the idea,
Elizabeth Spires has a poem called
"They Drive Through Childhood in Their Little Cars."
Henry Vaughan: 1621–1695.
Elizabeth Spires: born 1952.
Childhood: any and all dates apply.
Just what are those designs—
purposes, intentions, or patterns?
And why white?
The poet doesn't say.

II

The Gift

I took some thoughts and poured them out
and handed the full cups to you,
and each of them took on the shape
of what it had been poured into.

The contents were still warm and wet
but new dimensions had been set.
Once I had given these things away
they no longer belonged to me

but took the personality
of the recipient. And so
wrapped secrets pass from hand to hand,
a poem moves from mind to mind—

a gift consumable, renewed,
a helping of the Muses' food.

Lyric Leap

The fizzing spark, the lateral leap,
the sideways skitter (mind the gap!),
fugitive dream recalled mid-morning,
déjà vu pouncing without warning,
unexpected recollection,
serendipitous digression
meandering at an angle—pun
that stops you before you've begun,
tattered palimpsest, hapax,
puzzle that stymies you in your tracks,
lacuna, hiatus, sidebar,
sudden swerve, and you are far
along already toward surprise.
Pause a second and surmise.
Your destination was—where?
One sideways step may get you there,
your wings still crumpled, half-asleep—
one unassuming lyric leap.

Ovid's *Metamorphoses*

Speeded up dramatically,
the changes cinematically
unfold before our eyes. Their speed
doesn't allow the time we need
to take in details one by one.
What's happened to his hands? Her skin?
Tail, antlers, feathers—each excrescence
supersedes some human essence.
Agency, gestures—where are they?
Selves here do not fade away;
rather they're snuffed out suddenly.
Once Daphne's stiffened into tree,
all she can do is shake her hair—
her foliage—when Apollo's near.
The hero Perseus one by one
transforms his enemies to stone,
their postures frozen, rage and fear
petrified by the Gorgon's glare.
Actaeon calls, or tries to call,
his hounds; no voice comes out at all.
A stag at bay is what they sense;
we know the gory consequence.
Nobody has any choice;
they lose their bodies and their voice.
The pace of change, the loss of speech
are common features. But for each
individual transformation
there is a different motivation.
Envy, revenge, imprisonment,
lust, parody, or punishment—
some toxic cocktail blend of these
informs each metamorphosis.
But though the circumstances vary,
no transformation's temporary.
There's no undoing of the spell.
Might one exception prove the rule?

Io's transformed into a cow,
then back into a girl—one who
now fears her voice will be a moo.
How can Io not be cowed?
She hesitates to speak aloud,
and walking on two legs feels strange.
No one can wholly undo change.
As each fresh transformation's told,
we listeners long to be consoled,
reassured, as we read on.
But what is done can't be undone.
Stability is under threat.
Identity is in retreat.
Pulsating, writhing, never quiet
as shapes and appetites run riot,
this vivid pageantry, so easy
to enjoy, still leaves me queasy.
Beyond the borders of the text
I wonder what is coming next.
I close the book and put it down.
The nightmare images remain.

Under the Floorboards

Outside Bridgeport, the gold of afternoon
broke through clouds and factory chimneys. Brick
warehouses, pylons glowed
with late September light.
The blonde young woman sitting next to me
was taking notes in a copy of *Beloved*

and, skimmed from my light sleep, a dream came back:
two blonde little sisters in a barn.
Trespassing, hiding in the hayloft,
I overheard them weeping.
The dream was so close to the surface
it almost bumped its head on the dusty floorboards.

Nap

Our waking hours are stiff with the unsaid.
Sleep's feathery fingers tease
the carapace of silence.
A laugh erupts that started as a snore.

Muggy August afternoon, light rain
sparring with streaks of sun:
I am a cargo-laden barge, and am
the sluggish stream the barge is drifting down.

Messages

> *scissoring and mending*
> —James Merrill, "Yánnina"

Left on an uncleared restaurant table
scrawled on a cocktail napkin: FABLE.
Struggling to surface from a dream,
something keeps trying to get through.

Things are either what they seem
or else the opposite. The same
word can split and float apart.
Lord of the crossroads, oh Eshu,

since you look both ways, can you see
the many morphing into one
and the one scattering again?
The veil between the worlds is thin.

Something contrives to scramble through
a threshold garbled into myth.
In my notebook I make out
sensible little sister scrawled—

my writing, but I never wrote
those three words. From some other sphere
they took up mystic residence,
offering a Delphic sense

I laboriously decode.
The myth of dream, the truth of myth—
something keeps trying to break through.
And I wake up and turn to you.

Waking Up

I dreamed about a time I didn't know.
I dreamed about a place I'd never been.
It was the water. No, it was the air
blowing into the precinct of nightmare—
a nightmare shared. It was the wired war.
Wired, weird—how to separate?
Mine? All of ours? Whose was, whose is this city,
park, bench, bridge, railing, river?
Cherry trees, magnolias fling their arms,
wave their pink and white at us like banners,
and hustle us along the path of spring—
the haste, the taste, the hurry, and the crowd,
virus dripping off the trees, the dread
that clung to me as I climbed out of bed.

Tiger Stripes

Hiding, asleep, invisible
for hours in some mysterious cell,
the tiger cat emerges, yawning.
His stripes replicate the awning
of the Anxiety Hotel
where so many nights are spent.
After his interlude out of sight
curled up away from noise and light
someplace where no one could intrude
until he sauntered out for food,
the cat seems sleepy and content.

Camouflage stripes of gold and brown:
the tiger world is melting down.
Caught in a beam of morning sun,
massive transitions are going on,
each nation and each generation
vying for who will take possession
of the Hotel Anxiety
(who wants to manage it? Not me).
Who gets to stay? Who has to go?
Process laborious and slow.
Who moves ahead? Who stays behind?
Musclebound combatants grunt and grind.
Who's the owner? Who's the heir?
And will the fearful future care?

Striped camouflage of grey and black:
there's never any turning back.
Once the place is emptied out,
what was all the fuss about?
The fissures in the family,
the rivalry, the enmity:
door now ajar, each vacant suite,
blank windows staring at the street,
hotel abandoned, no life left—
we barely even feel bereft.

Camouflage stripes of grey and brown:
the tiger world is winding down.
Disruption on a local scale—
no one is forwarding the mail.
Shadows slide down a blank wall.
Our hotel is very small.
The stripes are vibrating: illusion,
the camouflage of our confusion.
The cat sits up and licks his paws.
We're all obedient to laws
too massive to assimilate.
It's still early. And it's late.

Brooding on Cities the Morning after a Cavafy Evening

Lavish accolades bestowed last night
upon a writer past their radiant reach
hailed him as *poet of cities*—whereupon
each borough preened and swelled from simple town
or mere municipality to polis,
metropolis, megalopolis, cosmopolis,
only to shrink back into an idea
(good poems somehow manage this) that fits
inside each reader's vision of a city.

On second thought, scratch *megalopolis*,
the clang and clatter of whose syllables
recalls, of all unlikely things, the Fifties
architecture that struck me today.
Years since I'd walked past the United Nations:
the stale and grimy veil of vague neglect
draping the hopeful, boastful shoebox buildings
ambitious for some polis of the future,
already shabby, ripe to be replaced.

Plato at the Crossroads

> *...I came upon a remarkable book in a garbage pile...it contained a set of dialogues by Plato.*
> —Roosevelt Montás, *Rescuing Socrates*

We were strolling up Broadway
last week, a brisk November day,
to do some errands, get some air,
and maybe look at furniture.
Approaching 125th Street,
we paused and waited for the light.
And as we stood there for a minute,
I spied a box. So what was in it?
Random stuff: boots, blue jeans, a book...
I bent to take a closer look.
The light turned green, then red again.
Between streetlight and a garbage can,
I glanced at what serendipity
or some blind chance had offered me.
This little book that I'd pulled out—
what would it prove to be about?
Three letters on the cover: A T O.
My first idea: cookbook? Potato?
Nope. Plato the philosopher
had been waiting for me here,
encased in a compact purple tome
which I proceeded to take home.
But not quite yet. There was still time
to look around for a living-room
sofa. Oh body yoked to soul!
Nobody's life is ever whole.
The mind may roam eternity;
the body whines: "What about me?
I'm flesh. I need a comfy seat."
You never know when you may meet
a philosopher in the street
to make the mixture more complete,

to help you bind the two together,
body and soul, in every weather.
Peripatetic—that was us,
until, footsore, we caught a bus.
But also Stoics equally,
as everyone these days needs to be.

Oracle of the everyday!
All that we see and yet pass by;
all that we pass and do not see—
abstraction in a patch of sun,
dream fragments buried before noon,
the silence reverie affords,
making room for (what else?) more words.
"Silence: a story people tell
or try to tell, but always fail,"
typed a student soundlessly
into the Chat the other day.
We only keep by giving away.
We always have to carve out space
for something else to find a place—
something ancient, also new.
It's better if we say goodbye
to books that we no longer need.
Leave them for someone else to read.
Who had discarded Plato? Why?
And was the book left there for me?

We tell a tale by passing it on
to we don't know who. We'll be gone,
but possibly where two roads cross
someone will notice as they pass,
pick up the book and take it home
and read the story one more time.

Sustainable Systems

Iphigenia walking toward the altar,
one long day and then so soon all over.
Which shall be our family of myth?
New moon. Wedding at sunset
against the backdrop of the Hudson River.
C. Diff? Murky malady. Ebola?
What calendar when there's no word for time?
The fall semester races toward a start,
the divorce crawls toward a settlement.
Visiting neighbor, cloudy forenoon:
carrots, zucchini, lettuce, onions,
heirloom tomatoes, ozone, acid rain.
Destroy the tunnels, they're rebuilt again.
Hummingbirds in the bee balm. Scattered showers.
What rubric, what barometer, what headline?
Slavers anchor in the harbor,
then go inland to ferret out their treasure.
What hoard, what hedge, what leverage, what barter?
Supermoon. The destruction of the Temple.
What liturgy? Dormition of the Virgin.
All rivers flow into the sea.
Barnet: Town Hall on the economy,
so distribution should undo excess.
What agency, what slogan, and what vision?
Water on fire. Elements. Hot stains.
On the brink where no solutions remain,
nothing sustainable's left to sustain,
what should we do? What shall we ever do?
Should we shut down
or turn away from the black crack to green
lawn and drowse away the afternoon?
Grass a flag of hopeful green stuff woven.
Green a blanket over the abyss.
Green a weave: renewal, pleasure, hope.
Day lilies. Shadows. Clouds float overhead.
What memory, what yardstick, what conclusion?

A slit of light under a closing door
and then no more?
One long day and then so soon all over?
Extinction, decimation, diachronic,
synchronic, syncretic, plague and cure.
Medium and message. Dislocation.
What trope, criterion, or iteration?
Theme and variation:
the slave ship anchors at the river's mouth.
Tunnels, tunnels branching underground.
Summer clouds sail slowly overhead.
Iphigenia paces toward the altar.

In Aulis: One Version

We live our lives along the in-between.
There is no clear-cut line, there is no border
to demarcate the unseen from the seen.

Here comes the princess, escorted by the queen.
Step down from the chariot, my daughter.
We live our lives along the in-between.

Iphigenia eagerly jumps down.
Let me go ahead and hug my father.
Between the unseen and the seen,

youthful innocence and beauty run.
This sleeping baby is her little brother.
We live our lives along the in-between.

In one of several sequels, having grown
into a man, Orestes kills his mother.
Between the seen and the unseen,

before the scarlet setting of the sun,
someone will lead the princess to an altar.
We live our lives along the in-between
zone that divides the seen from the unseen.

Among the Taurians

The reunion of Iphigenia and her brother
was the grain of sand
from which the early drafts emerged.
But with the patience poems can command,

"Among the Taurians" (its working title)
sat in a folder waiting
for several years. And when I fished it out
after this extended marinating,

the brother and the sister had receded
so far that they could be
dispensed with, like a ladder
no longer needed once you've climbed the tree.

Some vestiges remained.
The story went on beating like a heart.
The dramatis personae mattered less
than the template: together, then apart.

Separation/reunion/recognition:
the rhythm lingers as the figures blur.
Character plays a smaller role than plot,
said Aristotle. My students would concur.

The archetypal hero's journey home
everyone gets. Even if names are strange
(Eurykleia? Antinoos? Eumaios?),
the bones of the story do not change—

familiar, strange, and universal too.
Myth kitty, Larkin sneered. I disagree.
*Cross out, please, those immensely overpaid
accounts*, wrote Whitman, who refused to see

how—sturdy, versatile, resilient—
these old accounts keep paying dividends.
Meanings morph and split and realign
to new interpretations of old friends.

What drew me to this pair?
For one, I'd been translating their romance
(no more a tragedy than *The Winter's Tale*
or *The Tempest*); and two, the role of chance,

drawing the two together once again,
alive, determined, and against the odds
successful in their plot to get back home
when things seemed hopeless. Should we thank the gods?

So many ways of parsing each old tale.
Do not look for a moral here, I say
to students. Try to find a vision,
your own fresh take on this ancient play.

My early drafts, when I turn back to them,
look awful, both bombastic and austere,
too much, too little—nothing I would keep.
Still, the idea of that distant shore,

old trauma and perennial regret,
exile's lonely bed, bad dreams at dawn,
retain their power. I've retained the title:
"Among the Taurians." So we go on.

The Spark

That the retrievals reading can bestow
tend inward, backward, down, should come as no
surprise. To let yourself be carried, drawn
to first love, first idea, and on and on...
does reading happen any other way?
Of course it must. Yet every time I see
students and books connect, over and over
that spark, that arc, that leaping like a lover
makes me glad and grateful, reassured
a mind can find its echo in a word,
and story, stubborn, durable, somehow
exerts its magnetism even now.

Teaching the *Iliad*

I only thought of it the other day.
When we reached the *Iliad*, Book Three,
the theme emerged: responsibility,
how it's apportioned in a family:
unequal shares of worry, care, and labor.
I was reminded of our next-door neighbor,

his widowed mother and his feckless brother.
"Does Hector's situation sound familiar?
How much can, should we care for one another?"
I asked, sensing reaction in the room
(as far as one can gauge when one's on Zoom)
and weighing the dynamic we had seen

at the remove not only of a screen
but of an ancient poem (date—who knows?)
that eloquently tracks a family maze.
After class, I stood out on the lawn
(grass cold and wet with dew; September sun),
then paced and traced the labyrinth, turn by turn.

Teaching the Tigers

Arms folded, wearing tiger masks,
students sit. Questions? No one asks.

Loss and grief, exile, return:
how much of it can they take in?

The *Iliad*: to go to war.
The *Odyssey*: and come back home.

Epic's relentless forward motion,
lyric's gossamer attention,

adventure parsed as allegory,
the iterations of the story,

and then to choose the right translation
for a fearful generation.

May poetry keep finding ways
of piercing the miasmal haze

and reclaiming a clear space
behind each young and guarded face

and washing through the walls that hide
whatever's bubbling inside.

Fall semester's almost done.
Time to think ahead to spring.

The days will soon be getting longer.
The students go on getting younger.

The days will soon be getting longer.
The world and I are getting older.

The poems are untouched by age.
A fresh semester turns the page.

Who If I Cried

The seminar's purportedly
about poetry, so why

a massive art book on the table
open to a Gauguin plate?

The painter, born in 1848,
is currently undergoing cancellation—

process that may precede a death
or follow it, or maybe both.

The seminar is nearly over.
What is waiting around the corner?

Robert Lowell's poetry comes up
but it's late, we have to stop.

I think I hear a student say
"The younger poets—where are they?"

Two other students, heads together,
conspiratorially whisper.

I can catch the word *translation*.
Which is the target, which is the source?

We need translations, of course,
to bridge the space between generations—

a drastic, ever-widening gap.
And now the seminar table's top

turns slippery, treacherous: black ice.
I can hear my own raised voice:

Trying to talk to you guys is like
shouting across a mountain lake!

Who if I cried would hear me, though?
No one in this room right now.

The semester's nearly over.
What waits for us around the corner?

The black lagoon is cold and deep.
Visions bubble up through sleep.

The seminar room's now a vast hall,
huge paintings hanging on the wall.

To wash the grimy colors clean,
I take a hose to one of them

to restore its primal hue.
Morris Louis? Mark Rothko?

Can they have been cancelled too?
Who if I cried would hear? Below

the table, gleaming, icy, black:
the unfathomed mountain lake.

Gradus ad Parnassum

There was a hole in the ceiling
through which I had to climb
if I wanted to get to the next level.
A squarish hole, it looked impossibly small,
but I swung up one leg
and somehow squeezed the rest of my body through
and found myself on the roof of a high building.
On the rooftop: a playground full of children
much too involved in their games
to look up at an elderly newcomer.
Having reached the highest level,
I was invisible.

Liminal

Precisely as the most
memorable exchanges so
often occur at the brink
of departure, host and guest
both in the foyer, near the open door,
rocking from foot to foot, the rising roar
of the party still in full
swing behind the host,
who says or tries to say
goodbye to the departing
guest, who (wait! not yet!)
belatedly
remembers one last thing she meant to say,
or possibly
the pair of them both find themselves transfixed
by a shared uninvited memory
of someone who has not
been, who will not be
at this party
or any party ever again,
just that exchange at the threshold,
not an intentional permanent farewell,
only a provisional goodbye
(Happy New Year!) until we meet again,
although they know
though they do not say so
that this may be the last
meeting for host or guest
or any of us—
precisely
that liminality.

The Last Lecture Hall

Theaters that were never ours,
classrooms empty and refill.

We cross the stage and disappear.
Feverish categories blur.

Genre distinctions: what for?
The empty theater becomes

a lecture hall. A classroom morphs
into a forest murmuring

with voices. Words pelt down like rain
or rise like mist and dissipate.

Theater, classroom, maple, fir:
feverish categories blur,

presences pressing through the veil
of the phenomenal.

A leopard's padding down the aisle.
Tiger-masked students fill the seats

of the amphitheater.
The old professor, looking out

over the upturned faces, said
"You are all allegorical

figures to me. I will not learn
your names." Did the students laugh?

Tragedy, satire, comedy:
genres are deciduous.

Modes blur, leaves wither and fall.
The leaves of memory seemed to make

A mournful rustling in the dark.
(Longfellow, "The Fire of Drift-Wood")

Lights go on in the theater.
We stumble out. Class is over.

Tones of Meaning

> *Her tone of meaning but without the words.*
> —Robert Frost, "Never Again Would Birds' Song Be the Same"
>
> *He would cry out on life, that what it wants*
> *Is not its own love back in copy speech,*
> *But counter-love, original response.*
> —Robert Frost, "The Most of It"

The way that neutral empty space can shift
to desert desolation; or the way
solitude shades into loneliness
and silence can reverberate as echo,
an echo only emphasizing silence;
and how the space, the solitude, the silence
are charged with longing for another voice,
another presence even if unseen,
a presence that declares itself as voice,
presence as absence gently overheard,
add up to love. That solitary self
could be Adam in the bird-filled garden,
or any lover, or could be a child.
If a child's questions go unanswered, he
is likely to repeat them and repeat.
If the child knows her mother is close by,
somewhere in the garden out of sight,
close enough to hear her vital voice,
her tone of meaning but without the words,
that child feels safe. But if instead the mother
is peering at the window of a screen,
scanning small words without the tone of meaning,
words without the tone that gives them meaning,
the child is left unreassured, unanswered.
And words without the tone that gives them meaning
are all the solitary "he" who cried
for counter-love, original response
and not his own love back in copy speech,
hears in reply: a bot, a mocking echo.

Frost, who understood
empty space, desert places, the soft sound
somewhere in the garden out of sight
of the beloved's voice,
longed-for, elusive, and dependable,
failed to foresee the toneless syllables
marching across countless little tablets,
failed to imagine absence
and presence both as unavailable.

The Equation

Each day something will be asked of you.
And that's only the half of it:
someone will always want to give you something.
To give or not to give,
to take or not to take:
whichever choice you make,
a breath of satisfaction will blow past,
if only at having arrived at some decision—
satisfaction, though, laced with regret
you will remember and later on forget
unless, as years advance, a waking dream
unearths some part and brings it to the light.

Narrative's wet finger draws a line
down a loose pane that rattles
in the drafty window of your life.
History's face rises in the morning mist.
You peer out. It peers in.
Forces beneath the surface pulse and strain,
then take wing, escape to open air.
Recognition: payment of a debt
we forget, remember, and forget.
Morning, noon, and night,
life dapples dark, dark dapples light.
Give and take. Repeat.

Waiting in Line for the Disney Show

Metropolitan Museum

Waiting in line for the Disney show
is discipline in being slow.
Can these past years have taught us patience?
Having lined up for vaccinations
or tests in tents on a windy street,
shifting from foot to chilly foot—
such practice makes this echoing hall
the perfect place in which to stall.

The Disney show, presumably,
is what we're lined up here to see.
It closes soon! Don't waste a minute,
except the hour spent getting in it.
But the process of getting there
lavishes us with time to spare.
Stoically waiting here,
we have to focus on what's near.
Toddlers cast a doubtful eye
at high-relief sarcophagi;
one pokes a cautious finger in-
to a carved crevice in the stone.
Pony-tailed satyrs on a vase
caper as flute music plays.
Here's Hercules, his lion skin
slung round his neck like a cardigan
tied at the sleeves.
                          The Disney show
proves, when we get there, a grotto,
cavernous and dimly lit.
These galleries, though, where we wait
and inch along, are bathed in light.
A noonday slant of pale spring sun
picks out details and renders stone
fleshy and warm and palpable,

human in texture as in scale.
A marble head or arm or thigh:
normally we'd pass these by
without a second glance. Today
we have no power to walk away
from all the riches on display—
not least sun-kissed skin or stone—
before we duck back to a screen.
Yes, screens have been our medium for
a year and then another year.
But in the crowded gallery here
(social distances disappear),
masked and hopeful—here we are.

Visiting My Office 12/6/21

Twenty months since I was here.
Take down the faded calendar
stalled at March 2020.
My office is a small Pompeii,
surfaces ghostly, dusty, grey.
It all feels weary, flat, and stale.
Dead diplomas on the wall—
am I my own memorial?
Bulletin board with water stain—
did a cracked window let in rain?
Something certainly let in grit.
But no one cares if I do not.
Nobody cares. Nobody's here.
Up and down the hall I peer:
no voices, not one open door
here in Hill Hall on the fifth floor.
Why am *I* here? It's time to go.
Time has been moving fast and slow,
time has been moving slow and fast.
Keep what encapsulates the past.
Books on the shelves—okay. (But where
does the poetry inhere?
A question for another day.)
Coffee mug, hourglass—let them stay,
but throw the calendar away.
Yellowing handouts—out they go.
Out I go too. Not knowing when
or whether I'll come back again,
and stuffing underneath my mask
questions I might like to ask
and valedictions to it all,
I walk back down the empty hall.

Ghost Guest

I sometimes think I recognize the face
of my own death. Knowing it is nearer
makes me feel it ought to be familiar,
a neutral guest I've seen somewhere before.
Even if it's not a face I know,
can it be ignored,
that shadow presence quiet in a corner?
And therefore as a stranger give it welcome.
Which is the lesser of two evils here,
which the least boorish way to be a host?
Who is hosting whom? If I'm a host,
I'm also just as much a guest, a ghost.
What heart heard of, ghost guessed. So,

death, I'll acknowledge you, I'll be polite,
hand you a drink and let you circulate
and talk with others. You will cycle back.
Precisely: *at my back I always hear*
and do not hear and see and do not see,
know and do not know you'll catch up with me.
Since I think I know you from somewhere,
why should I be so sure
that you do not know me at least as well,
my length of days and my Achilles heel,
which in each person's in a different place?
Sometimes I think I recognize your face.

A War by Any Other Name

a war by any other name
the darkness and the light extreme
and are the wars not all the same
hands reach out and try to hold
the stretch the bonds the arms enfold
masks sheltering us from the cold
virus pushing us together
virus pulling us apart
is our time too late for art
what is the point of poetry
poets when asked say Don't ask me
we try to hold to it and see
heroism fear defiance
get vaccinated trust the science
the roaring crowd whom to believe
late in life I fell in love
poems passed from friend to friend
hinge and pivot hand to hand
flashes of warmth hold off the end
light and darkness both extreme
rusty black and golden gleam
a war by any other name
father mother child translation
families huddle in the station
tightening our human bond
a theater rubbled by a bomb
hospital art school targeted
as if a blister swelled and bled
and burst the septic dark the light
today the same length as tonight
I try to teach the Trojan war
tell me what they were fighting for
is every war the same the same
evil with a different name
the darkness and the light extreme
remember and forget again

Acknowledgments

Thanks to the following publications, where some of these poems have appeared: *Bad Lilies, Bosque, Classical Outlook, Common Knowledge, Crab Orchard Review, Gettysburg Review, Ha-aretz, Hopkins Review, Hudson Review, Liber Review, Literary Matters, Los Angeles Review of Books, The New Criterion, The New Yorker, Plume, Raritan, Southwest Review, Times Literary Supplement, Upstreet, Women's Review of Books.*

"Forest and Trees" appeared in *Tree Lines: 21st Century American Poems*, edited by Jennifer Barber, Jessica Greenbaum, and Fred Marchant (Grayson Books, 2022).

RACHEL HADAS is the author of many collections of poetry, most recently *Pandemic Almanac* (2022) and *Love and Dread* (2021). A selection of her prose, *Piece by Piece,* was published in 2021. She has translated Euripides' *Helen* and his two Iphigenia plays, and she was one of many translators of *Tales of Dionysus* (2022), a lengthy epic by the 5th century CE poet Nonnus. Rachel Hadas is Professor Emerita at Rutgers University-Newark, where she taught in the English Department for many years. Rachel's honors include a Guggenheim Fellowship in Poetry, the O. B. Hardison Award in Poetry from the Folger Shakespeare Library, and an award in literature from the Academy-Institute of Arts and Letters.

www.ingramcontent.com/pod-product-compliance
Lightning Source LLC
Chambersburg PA
CBHW021022090426
42738CB00007B/866